CRAZY INVENTIONS

Jeannette Fidell and Tom Funk

SCHOLASTIC BOOK SERVICES

New York Toronto London Auckland Sydney Tokyo

ISBN: 0-590-31329-0

12 11 10 9 8 7 6 5 4 3 2 1   11   0 1 2 3 4 5/8

Printed in the U. S. A.   06

Introduction

There is an old saying, "Necessity is the mother of invention." This means that when someone feels a strong need for something, that's when the spark that leads to a great new gadget gets ignited. Sometimes the invention is breathtakingly simple, while others are crazily complicated.

The crazy inventions assembled here are all *real*. Someone actually dreamed up and received a patent for each one of them. Whether any of them were ever commercially produced, or of any use to anyone besides the inventor, is very questionable. Whether any are really practical is very doubtful. One thing they all are is silly.

So, if "Necessity is the mother of invention," here's a whole family of wacky offspring you'll probably never have any use for at all—except to make you laugh.

This double armchair serves a double purpose. The woman can listen while the man can holler away. It helps if the listener is hard of hearing.

CLICK

Some people are camera-shy. This invention makes it possible to take photographs through a hat without being noticed. Of course, you may have to explain why your hat clicks.

This rain cover protects your hair and your hat. Notice that it protects your face as well as your back. The faucet in back carries the water sufficiently away from your shoulders and back, so that it leaks directly into your boots. The inventor didn't quite go far enough with this one.

This invention serves two purposes: It is a parlor ornament and conversation piece at the same time. It is also a device to get rid of rats and mice without using deadly poisons. The figure of the cat is drawn on heavy cardboard with several coats of illuminating paint. Piercing phosphorus eyes shine in the dark and scare the mice and rats. And this cat never needs its litter changed!

Who suffers more, the snorer who wakes up in the morning with a dry throat or the listener who is kept awake all night? This is an anti-snoring mouthpiece with valves to control the volume of air from the lungs and a muffler to dampen the sound. Doesn't look too comfortable, however.

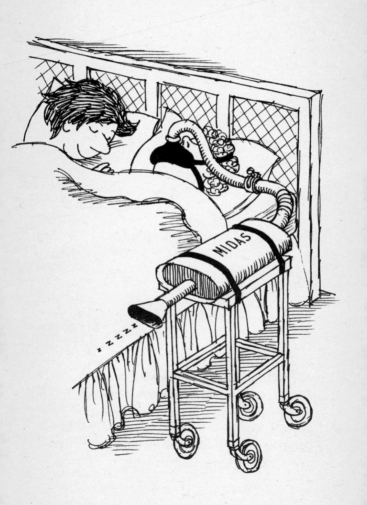

This invention was devised for heavy sleepers or people with defective hearing. It is a burglar alarm which drops a bucket of water over the sleepers. By opening and entering the window, the burglar triggers the pail of water. Not for people who can't swim.

This TALKING WATCH was devised for office workers who are clock-watchers. This timepiece is capable of calling out the hours. It would be an excellent invention if it could only tell the correct time.

This PORTABLE HAMMOCK hooks over
the back of a seat and over the top of the seat
ahead. It allows a train traveler to rest his head
and dangle his legs through a hole in the bottom
of the hammock.

Rude, flirtatious men have been around for a long time. This device was attached to a woman's underskirt. It had a sharp point which protruded in response to unwanted pressure by a masher. A very "tack-ful" way of saying no.

This is called a VELOCIPED SHOWER BATH. It combines washing your face with a means of keeping in shape. The power created by pedaling is used to drive a rotating pump that forces the water up from a tank. The harder one pedals, the more powerful the flow of water. A heater can also be placed below the water tank, making it possible to take a hot shower. It could be the answer for people too rushed to shower and exercise separately.

This invention promises onions without tears. A transparent plastic bag is placed inside a window in which a person can peel onions without being bothered by the fumes. The hands, the onion, and the knife can be inserted through a pair of tubular plastic mittens. Also good for cracking rotten eggs, if you are so inclined.

Want to play a duet and can't find a partner? This PIANO-CELLO invention is meant for the musician who is versatile enough to play the piano with the left hand and the cello with the right hand. If the musician can sing, she can be a one-person orchestra.

This invention is a LIFE PRESERVER. The top part consists of a floating buoy in which the wearer has freedom to move his head and arms. It provides sufficient power to float and also gives complete shelter. A month's supply of food and drinking water can be stored in the upper section. The cover can be closed when the high seas are running. It provides protection from voracious fish who do not own their own can openers.

This is another device for those who have been shipwrecked. A cartridge-inflated balloon allows a person to stay afloat indefinitely. It can also be used by anyone who likes to float without tiring their arms and legs, or is just too lazy to even float on their own power.

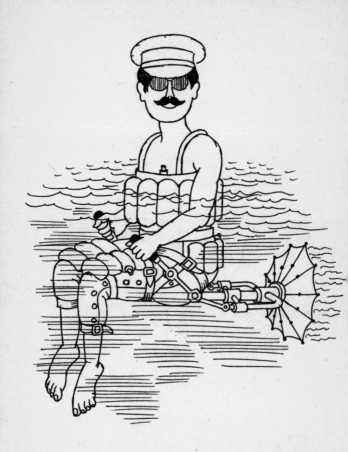

For those who can't learn to swim, this device may be the solution. It has two handles to move backward and forward, and an India-rubber suit provides the necessary buoyancy. Not to be used in swimming meets.

Some people who walk their dogs at night need to be reminded to bring their pooper-scoopers with them. This CURB YOUR DOG sign is projected on the sidewalk through a lighted reflector mirror at night. Unfortunately, not too many dogs can read.

Professional golfers look so smooth that amateur golfers try to imitate the way they swing their clubs. In this invention the golfer's feet are strapped to foot plates and his head is in a cap with a chin piece. He wears a belt with three rods attached. The club is gripped by a boom that guides the swing. The machine gets an integrated motion by guiding the player's hands, wrists, arms, head, shoulders, hips, knees, and feet. It even prevents the player from turning his head until after the ball is struck. The pity is that the machine can't be used on the golf course.

A gentleman should tip his hat when he meets a lady. But what does a gentleman do when his hands are occupied with bundles? This invention provides the solution.

Have you ever been asked to lend a hand? This EXTRA HAND invention is a device for holding the bowl steady while the cook mixes in the other ingredients. Very hand-y.

This invention carries food from the kitchen to the dinner table. Fast food right in your home.

A HANDBAG ALARM was designed to foil muggers. When the handbag is snatched or dropped it activates a horn that yells BEEP! YOW! Of course, it would help if the victim yelled too.

This PROTECTO-CANE is an anti-mugging device. It consists of a tube, made of aluminum or wood, to which a smoke-alarm buzzer and a red pilot light is attached. A tiny slide switch activates the light and the alarm, which shrieks like a banshee and cannot be turned off until the umbrella handle is unscrewed and a reset switch is pushed.

This SURPRISE TRAPDOOR invention is meant to foil bank robbers. A button is placed on the inside of a cashier's position to be pressed if a robber shows up. This might help the number of robberies to "fall off" after a while.

This NOISELESS ALARM was designed to make direct communication between the sleeper and a clock. It was meant to be used by considerate people who do not want to disturb others.

This horn-shaped ventilator was designed to filter fresh air into stuffy Victorian bedrooms. The inventor went broke after customers complained of cracking their heads when raising them.

Some people are such heavy sleepers that even alarm clocks do not awaken them. This invention is for them. Getting thrown out of bed is accomplished by a tilting mechanism activated by a powerful spring. The spring is released by setting a clock to the hour you wish to get up — literally.

This milkmaid has a milking stool strapped around her waist so she can carry two pails and a place to sit down at the same time. It might be a useful item for standing in line at rock concerts, waiting to buy tickets.

This invention is a device for girls who think that dimples make them look cute and attractive. Unfortunately, while it may give you dimples, you also may look like your head's been caught in a pair of tongs. But some people will do anything to look different.

These eyeglasses go over a chicken's head and around the back of its neck, not to improve the chicken's vision, but to protect his eyes from pecks by other fowls. Very famous chickens might wear sunglasses to protect their identity as well as their eyes.

This is an ENERGY SAVER. Instead of using a thermostat hooked to the furnace, this window closer is attached to a clock timer which closes the window at a specified time. It's good for windows that can't tell time.

This SERPENTINE PEDALPHONE was designed for the musician who can read music, play the correct notes, and steer the vehicle at the same time. Who could ask for anything more?

This is a three-in-one CONVERTIBLE BEDROOM PIANO. You can store your socks and underwear in the wardrobe drawers, you can sleep in it, and if you wake up in the middle of the night you can play Beethoven, boogie-woogie, or rock and roll . Also, when you are thrown out of your house for disturbing the peace, you are already packed.

This FAMILY BICYCLE was built for five. It was designed to carry a weight of over 400 pounds. It does nothing to protect the pedaler from extreme exhaustion, nor from children who wish to go in five different directions.

If you ever had the misfortune to have grapefruit juice sprayed into your eye, you would welcome this invention of a grapefruit shield.

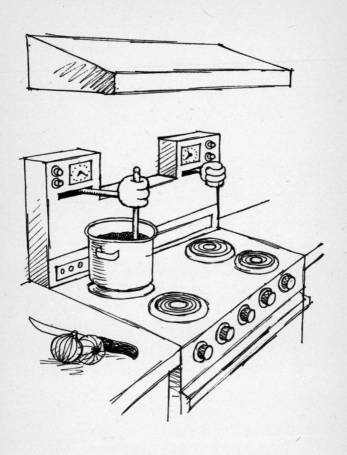

An AUTOMATIC STIRRER was invented for puddings, cereals, etc. It allows the cook to be free to do other things, like break dishes and drop eggs on the floor.

This is a device for giving a baby a BUMP-LESS RIDE. The front wheel is attached to a series of springs which rise and fall with the steps. Of course, babies who love to be bumped may feel deprived and cry a lot.

This invention is a bribe to get children to take castor oil or bitter-tasting medicine. After swallowing the medicine, the child can then eat the chocolate spoon. If the child hates chocolate, you're in trouble.

This DOMESTIC MOTOR was designed for a person who likes to do many things at the same time. This lady is knitting socks, rocking the cradle in front, swinging the swing in back, washing clothes, and churning butter. All she has to do is sit and use the rocking chair.

Every package of cigarettes sold in the U.S. has the following notice printed on it:

WARNING! THE SURGEON GENERAL HAS DETERMINED THAT CIGARETTE SMOKING IS DANGEROUS TO YOUR HEALTH.

This box of cigarettes goes one step further than the Surgeon General. It coughs and hacks when a cigarette is removed.

Some smokers' eyes become irritated by
smoke. This device helps to carry the smoke
away from the face and eyes. An easier solution
would be to quit smoking.

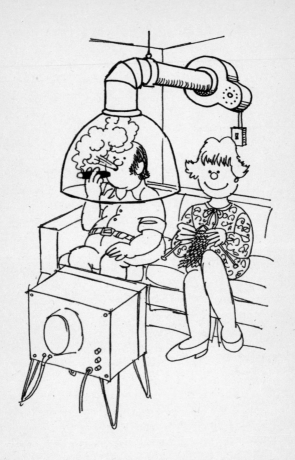

This is an invention for the family that enjoys sitting together. They can watch TV together while she knits and he smokes a cigar. The exhaust fan is a transparent dome which carries the cigar smoke to the outside.